DIALOGUE ON CONSCIOUSNESS

Minds, Brains, and Zombies

DIALOGUE ON CONSCIOUSNESS

Minds, Brains, and Zombies

John Perry

Hackett Publishing Company, Inc.
Indianapolis/Cambridge

21 20 19 18   1 2 3 4 5 6 7

For further information, please address
    Hackett Publishing Company, Inc.
    P.O. Box 44937
    Indianapolis, Indiana 46244-0937

    www.hackettpublishing.com

Cover design by Deborah Wilkes
Composition by Aptara, Inc.

Library of Congress Cataloging-in-Publication Data

Names: Perry, John, 1943– author.
Title: Dialogue on consciousness : minds, brains, and zombies /
    John Perry.
Description: Indianapolis : Hackett Publishing Company, Inc.,
    2018. | Includes bibliographical references.
Identifiers: LCCN 2018006879| ISBN 9781624667367 (pbk.) |
    ISBN 9781624667374 (cloth)
Subjects: LCSH: Consciousness—Miscellanea. | Imaginary
    conversations.
Classification: LCC B808.9 .P48 2018 | DDC 128/.2—dc23
LC record available at https://lccn.loc.gov/2018006879

The paper used in this publication meets the minimum re-
quirements of American National Standard for Information
Sciences—Permanence of Paper for Printed Library Materials,
ANSI Z39.48–1984.

∞

CONTENTS

INTRODUCTION

Gretchen Weirob, Sam Miller, and Dave Cohen are my inventions. Gretchen teaches at a small college, Dave is a student there, and Sam is a local minister. I think of them as having a life beyond these *Dialogues*, however, that explains how they came to be written.

When Weirob, Miller, and Cohen had philosophical conversations, Miller kept fairly detailed notes. He wrote up these notes in a rather dry fashion, which focused on the arguments. Dave Cohen gave me a lot of information about how the conversations actually went, and, of course, I have my own memories of Gretchen Weirob and Sam Miller. These are the sources I have used to reconstruct this dialogue and its two companions, *A Dialogue on Personal Identity and Immortality*, and *Dialogue on Good, Evil, and the Existence of God*. I found the notes of the conversations presented here in a folder of Miller's that mainly consisted of works by and about Leibniz. That struck me as a bit odd, but turned out to have an explanation. I'm still searching for more notes from their conversations.

This story doesn't explain one rather puzzling thing. From events in the other *Dialogues*, we know these notes must come from a conversation no later than the early 1970s. Yet Gretchen, Sam, and Dave talk about topics, and use terminology, that became common in philosophy much later, like "the zombie argument" and "the knowledge argument." It's almost as if they had read David Chalmers, *The Conscious Mind*. It seems that the three of them were so brilliant that they came up with ideas, and terminology, years before it appeared elsewhere. That is the only explanation I can think of.

MONDAY

Gretchen Weirob welcomes Sam Miller and Dave Cohen for lunch and philosophical discussion.

MILLER: Something smells good!

WEIROB: Tomato soup. From fresh tomatoes, not a can. Enjoy!

Let's make sure I have our plan straight. Dave has the week off for spring break; he doesn't have to attend classes. And I have the week off; I don't have to teach classes. As a minister, Sam can pretty much do what he wants with his time, except on Sundays and when he has a christening or a funeral. So we are going to meet here Monday, Wednesday, and Friday to talk philosophy over lunch. I'll provide the food, you guys provide the topics.

MILLER: My job is a *bit* more demanding than that, Gretchen. But I'm looking forward to lunch and philosophy.

WEIROB: No offense intended.

So what's our topic today?

1

COHEN: Sam and I have been talking about René Descartes*.[1]

WEIROB: You are trying to convince Sam he isn't dreaming? Or he is trying to convince you? Or perhaps he is trying to convince you that one of Descartes' arguments for the existence of God really works?

MILLER: None of those things really. Dave is trying to show me that Descartes' arguments for dualism don't work. I'm resisting. I like Descartes' arguments. Especially his conclusion.

WEIROB: Cartesian dualism, huh? The mind is one thing, completely immaterial. The body, including the brain, is a very complicated physical object. We each have a mind and a body, until we die.

            I'm not surprised you like Descartes' views, Sam. He thinks our bodies are material objects, doomed to return to dust and ashes. But our minds are immaterial. They can't fall apart, because minds have no parts. Such immaterial minds are good candidates for immortal souls.

MILLER: You are exactly right. I think I have, or perhaps that I am, an immaterial immortal soul. So Descartes' way of looking at it is very attractive to me.

            I assume you don't think this, Gretchen. You're happy to think that you're just a physical being.

---

1. An * indicates that information about the author or work mentioned in the text can be found in the Bibliography. Additional reading suggestions can also be found there.

I don't want to be just a physical thing. I don't really understand why anybody would be happy merely being a physical being.

Admit it, Gretchen, deep down wouldn't you like to be immaterial and so possibly immortal? Then the three of us could continue to have these conversations in heaven someday!

WEIROB: I admit, that would be nice, assuming we all end up in heaven, which isn't so obvious in my case. If we are simply immaterial souls in heaven, you wouldn't have a mouth and I wouldn't have ears, so conversaton might be difficult, but I suppose there is some more direct way of communicating in heaven. Actually, immortality might be a bit much. But maybe a few extra years of disembodied philosophical discussions would be fun. And perhaps I could learn to play a harp. Except if it is just my immaterial soul that survives, without any hands, that might be tricky.

MILLER: Sarcasm. I had a feeling you'd say something like that. You are such a materialist.

WEIROB: I plead guilty to being a materialist. But we need to be careful here. Some materialists are "eliminative materialists." They think minds were part of a theory humans came up with a long time ago, when they didn't know better. Minds were immaterial things of some sort. Now that we know how the brain and central nervous system work, we should just reject the theory, and "eliminate" minds altogether. Nineteenth-century chemists had a theory that included phlogiston, a special substance that explained fire. Now we realize there is no such stuff, and the phenomenon of things catching fire can be better explained without it. Eliminative materialists think our concept of mind has the same status. We should put it in the dustbin and just talk about brains.

MILLER: So if you aren't an eliminative materialist, what sort of materialist are you?

WEIROB: I think minds are more like stars. Our ancestors noticed stars and learned a lot about them. They observed constellations. They learned to navigate with the North Star. But they didn't know what stars were....

MILLER: Confucius said that stars were holes in the sky from which the light of the infinite shines....

WEIROB: That's an impressive bit of knowledge, Sam! So Confucius was right that there were stars, and he probably had names for many stars and for the constellations. But he had a very incorrect idea about what stars were.

COHEN: I get your point. When we learned that stars were distant firey objects, and not holes in the sky, we didn't eliminate stars and all we had learned about them from our thinking. We just understood them better. You think minds are like stars and not like phlogiston.

WEIROB: Exactly. It turns out that minds are not immaterial, but just brains. But we learned a lot about them even while not realizing what they really were. We developed a huge vocabulary for thinking about the thoughts, beliefs, desires, illusions, and so on. We don't need to eliminate any of this now that we know—or at least I think we know—that they are basically brains. Maybe we can improve it, because we're just recently in a position to understand minds better.

MILLER: You are a noneliminative materialist, but still a materialist. Still seems absurd to me.

WEIROB: Actually I prefer the term "physicalist." I'm a noneliminative physicalist. But that name won't make my view seem less absurd to you, Sam!

MILLER: You are right about that.

WEIROB: But look, I have an open mind. Maybe you can convince me of dualism. What are Descartes' arguments? Strike that—I don't want a list. Just give us his best argument.

MILLER: That argument starts in the first two *Meditations*, and goes on through the sixth—the last—*Meditation*. Descartes doubts the existence of the whole material world, including his own body. He might be dreaming, or perhaps an evil demon is fooling him into thinking there is a material world.

COHEN: Then we get *cogito ergo sum*—"I think, therefore I exist."

WEIROB: He doesn't really say that in the *Meditations*, Dave. That's from the *Discourse on Method*.

MILLER: Well, whatever. He says things to the same effect. His point is that even if he suspends belief in the whole material world, he can't doubt that he exists. He must exist even if he is only dreaming, or an evil demon is fooling him with the illusion that there is an external world full of material objects.

WEIROB: Some philosophers don't even think he got that right. All he had a right to say is "thoughts exist" or something like that. But I'll let that pass.

MILLER: Thank you.

COHEN: Just to show that I know my *Meditations*, even though I had the quote's source wrong, let me tell you what comes next. He asks what this *I*, the existence of which he can't doubt, amounts to. Since he doubts that his body can exist, but can't doubt that *he* thinks, and so exists, he concludes that he is essentially a mind. And what he can't doubt about himself and his mind is that it thinks, imagines, remembers, and perceives—or at least seems to.

MILLER: Quite right. He thinks that his mind—which he takes to be his soul—can exist, even if his body, including his brain, doesn't exist. From that he concludes that the mind—the thing that thinks, imagines, perceives, and the like—is not a material thing. It's not extended—it doesn't take up space. Taking up space is the *essence* of material objects. They don't think. Thinking—being conscious—is the *essence* of minds. Minds are not extended.

WEIROB: That seems to show, at best, that he doesn't *know* that the mind is a material thing. He can doubt that it's a material thing. But we can't go from *not* knowing that the mind is material, and being able to doubt it, to knowing that it's *not* material.

COHEN: You called that the "fallacy of misplaced nega- tion" once in class. I do *not* know that Topeka is the capital of Kansas. For all I know it might be Wichita. But that doesn't mean I know that Topeka is *not* the capital of Kansas.

WEIROB: Exactly right. Descartes' argument seems to com- mit the fallacy of misplaced negation. Just for the record, though, Topeka *is* the capital of Kansas.

MILLER: We have to be fair to Descartes here. He doesn't claim, in these early parts of the *Meditations*, to have *proven* that the mind is not a material object. He's just established the possibility. He leaves the conclusion until the last *Meditation*, the sixth. By then he has shown, or thinks he has shown, that an all-powerful God created and runs the universe. That God, being benevolent, won't fool us as long as we are careful....

WEIROB: Actually, it's never been clear to me why a com- pletely benevolent God would want to fool us, even if we *are* careless....

MILLER: Can we leave that for another day, Gretchen?

            As I was saying, we carefully consider our mind and its operations—thinking, imagining, perceiv- ing, and so on. We don't notice anything material going on. We carefully study the body and brain, and we don't notice anything like a thought or an image, just material processes. From all this, Descartes thinks we have a right to conclude that the mind is one thing, whose essence is thinking, and the brain something quite different, whose essence is being extended, taking up space, just like any other material object. While alive, a human is a combination of the two, but what is essential is the mind, which can survive death.

WEIROB: But if we don't accept all of Descartes' deep thinking about the certain existence of an all-perfect God, aren't we still just where we were at the end of the second *Meditation*? The mind doesn't seem very much like a brain, and the brain doesn't seem very much like a mind. So what? Superman doesn't seem to be very much like Clark Kent. But, in fact, they are one and the same. Maybe I shouldn't say "in fact" with regard to fictional superheroes. But you get my point.

MILLER: I didn't expect you to accept the God part, Gretchen. For Descartes, proving the existence of God removes his reasons for doubting the existence of the external world, and so restores his faith in his senses. I assume you have your own reasons for not doubting the external world, and trusting your senses. But given that you do trust them, don't you readily infer that things with radically different properties, as different as a pain or a thought or a whole mind, and a convoluted lump of gray stuff, aren't the same? After all, it seems to me Superman and

Clark Kent have a lot in common, compared to my brain and my mind. They are both visible, tangible, speak English, and alike. Lois and Jimmy would certainly be surprised to learn that Clark was Superman. But it wouldn't seem absurd as it would be if Clark turned out to be a number. But it seems to me that the mind being the brain is just about that absurd.

WEIROB: But your mind and your brain *do* have a lot in common. Your mind is surely not an abstract object, like a number. Both the mind and the brain are part of the "causal realm." They change, and their changes have causes and effects. Your mind and your brain are both affected by the external world when you perceive. Both are involved in causing your actions. When you decide to do something, you form an intention, your mind changes. According to dualists like Descartes, this has an effect on your brain. Your brain changes in ways that affect your nervous system, muscles, and so on, causing your limbs or your mouth or whatever to move, in ways that will put your intention into effect. Doesn't this suggest that there is just one thing, with two names, "the mind" and "the brain"?

MILLER: But look. If you follow Clark Kent around all day, eventually you will see him duck into a phone booth and put on his cape and tights and the rest. If you observe him carefully, that is, you will see that one single thing does have Superman's characteristic properties as well as Clark Kent's. So you can conclude there is only one person.

But it seems to me however carefully you inspect a brain, you won't find a thought or an image there. And however carefully you pay attention to your mind while thinking, you won't find a mass of gray matter. The brain and the mind are certainly coordinated; as Descartes says, they are constantly interacting. When you see something, what happens in your eyes and brain causes what happens in the mind. When you act, your decision or volition in the mind causes changes in the brain, and then in the rest of the body, resulting in movements. But that doesn't make them the same.

COHEN: Leibniz* gave you some help here, Sam. Leibniz imagines enlarging a brain so it is big enough to walk around in. No matter how carefully you inspect what is going on, he says, all you will see is material structures doing material things. I suppose nowadays he would say that all you will see is chemical and electrical activity in a big maze of neurons and axons and the like. But you won't see a thought, or a mental image, or an emotion.

WEIROB: Another philosopher, A. C. Ewing*, makes the point this way. He suggests that if you're a materalist, you should grab a red-hot piece of iron. You will experience a severe throb of pain. If you carefully reflect on the throb of pain, you will surely notice that it isn't like anything you would *see* if you were looking at a brain.

COHEN: A little passive-aggressive, I would say.

WEIROB: I thought Sam might like that.

MILLER: Well, not really. I don't want you materialists to suffer. I just want you to repent and give up your amazingly implausible view.

COHEN: That all reminds me of something a little less erudite than Leibniz or Ewing—a movie you may have seen, *Fantastic Voyage*.

MILLER: I sort of remember it. Raquel Welch was in it, and Arthur Kennedy.

WEIROB: It's a great movie. It has a perfectly believable Cold War plot. A Russian scientist comes over to the West with an important secret to divulge. But before he can divulge it, he has a stroke.

MILLER: That's right. The usual procedure would be to aim a laser at the blood clot responsible for the stroke and dissolve it or explode it or whatever. But they think that if they do this, they will probably destroy the part of the brain that holds the important secret information. They don't want to do that.

COHEN: So they do the obvious thing. They put Raquel Welch and Arthur Kennedy and a laser gun into a submarine. Then they shrink the submarine and everything in it down to the size of a grain of sand, or smaller, and inject it into the scientist's bloodstream. Their mission is to travel up the bloodstream to the injured part of the brain, and use their miniaturized laser gun to blast the clot in a precise shot that won't affect the important information held in nearby parts of the brain.

MILLER: A great movie. I have a clear memory of Raquel Welch in her latex jumpsuit, looking beautiful and scientific at the same time.

WEIROB: I didn't think men of the cloth noticed such things.

MILLER: Well, surprise, we do.

So, Dave, I suppose your point is that it's like Arthur and Raquel were inside a brain as large as a factory, except that the brain is normal size and they are tiny.

COHEN: Exactly. As you recall, Arthur Kennedy and Raquel Welch have many adventures on their way to the blood clot. For one thing, they take the wrong fork at one point and end up in the inner ear, which is very noisy. But there are also some pleasant parts of their voyage. During one of these, as they are gliding through the brain in their submarine, they look out of the window of the submarine at the amazing scene the scientist's brain presents to them. They see some bluish bubbling in the distance.

MILLER: I think I remember that.

COHEN: Arthur Kennedy puts his arm around Raquel Welch and says, "Look. That's a thought. We are the first people ever to see a thought!" So here they are, in basically the situation Leibniz imagined, but they don't see anything strange about seeing a thought.

MILLER: Are you sure you have that right? I don't think submarines have windows.

COHEN: Well, of course I'm not sure I have it right! For crying out loud, this is a philosophy discussion, not an oral exam in modern cinema. Maybe they were looking out of a periscope. But I have it basically right. Kennedy says something like that, and Raquel Welch finds it perfectly normal.

MILLER: That *was* a great movie. But if Leibniz or Ewing were in the submarine with Arthur and Raquel, they surely would not have agreed. Perhaps Ewing would say, "You guys are seeing the physical correlate of a thought, very possibly the cause of the thought. But you are not seeing the thought itself." Who are we going to believe? Astute philosophers like Ewing and Leibniz? Or Arthur Kennedy and Raquel Welch?

WEIROB: Suppose I accept the point that you and Leibniz and Ewing are making. That doesn't *force* us to say that the mind is not the brain. We *could* simply conclude that, in addition to their physical properties, brains have *nonphysical* properties. We can't *see* these properties when we look at brains, but if we have brains, we *experience* them. We aren't forced to accept Descartes' conclusion, that the mind is one thing, and the brain is another. At most we have to accept that the brain has nonphysical *properties* of some sort.

COHEN: You are suggesting that Aruthur and Raquel and Leibniz and Ewing could compromise. They could agree that they are seeing a thought, and would even see an intense pain, if the scientist were to awake and grab a red-hot poker while they were in his brain. But they would not see the properties that *made* the event they saw a thought or a pain.

Here is an analogy of sorts. You might hear a criminal say, "I was at home in bed when the robbery occurred." The event you are seeing is a lie, but you don't see the facts that make it a lie. So, maybe it's a bit like that. Arthur and Raquel see a thought, but they can't see the properties that *make* what they see a thought.

MILLER: I see that there is room for such a compromise. But I'm not sure I see the point. Gretchen, suppose you were willing to compromise and admit that pains and emotions and thoughts and decisions are nonphysical, in that these events have nonphysical properties that are essential to what they are. Why wouldn't you go further and simply accept Descartes' conclusion? If there were nonphysical properties, wouldn't it be reasonable that the things that have them and the events that involve them, are also nonphysical?

COHEN: I'm not so sure. Historically, long before very much was known about brains, a lot of philosophers thought the weak part of Descartes' picture was the mind and the body were two things that causally interacted. There was a brilliant princess....

WEIROB: Princess Elizabeth of Bohemia.*...

COHEN: Yes, Princess Elizabeth. She corresponded with Descartes about this. She said that it didn't make sense for a physical object to have an effect on an immaterial object, something with no extension, because physical objects have effects on each other through *contact*. They bump into each other. Or physical light rays bounce off of them, which affect the eyes. Or they produce sound waves that affect the ears, and so on. But how would any of this affect the mind, if minds are immaterial and unextended? You can't bump into an immaterial object. Even the smallest particle or the most powerful wave can't very well affect something that is unextended, can it?

WEIROB: Princess Elizabeth also couldn't see how an immaterial object, like Descartes took the mind to be, could affect a physical object, like the brain. Maybe she would have found it a bit more intelligible, if it were simply the physical and nonphysical properties of the same thing interacting.

MILLER: Well, Princess Elizabeth made some very interesting points, I guess. But Descartes must have had good answers.

WEIROB: Not ones that convinced much of anyone. The problem of interaction was actually a big crisis in philosophy. Many philosophers couldn't accept that part of Descartes' picture and wanted to avoid dualism. Some advocated materialism. But a number of rather brilliant philosophers turned to idealism.

MILLER: Like Berkeley*, I guess. He said the physical world was really all mental, just patterns of ideas.

Sort of a shared illusion—although he wouldn't have put it that way.

COHEN: I think of Berkeley's view like this. God and humans are sharing a video game. God is in control of the game, but allows us to make moves. He doesn't need any electronics to do this. It's a very good game, so, at least until we read Berkeley, we think we are in touch with a world of mind-independent things. Of course, Berkeley wouldn't call it all a game!

MILLER: What's a video game?

COHEN: I'll show you later.

WEIROB: You can show me, too. Sam and I are from a different era, Dave. If we play a game, it's usually bridge, or gin rummy.

Leibniz had a similar view that was in some ways similar to Berkeley's. He thought the world consisted of a lot of minds, or mindlike things—maybe an infinity of them, I'm not sure. He called them monads. God arranges things so their states are all synchronized, as if there were a physical world they were all perceiving in common from different perspectives. As you say, sort of a shared illusion. Or a shared video game, I guess. But with no real interaction between bodies, which are part of the illusion, and minds, which are not.

MILLER: And all of this was to avoid the problem of interaction?

WEIROB: That would be an oversimplification. But it's sort of right.

MILLER: I'd love to understand Leibniz, but it probably won't happen in this lifetime. And I must admit I like Berkeley. But I don't think you are going to be convinced by his arguments for idealism. So maybe we can also set Berkeley aside, at least for now. . . .

COHEN: So where does that leave us?

MILLER: I admit that interaction is a problem. But it really seems that Ewing's point was right. So perhaps I should just stick with the position Gretchen suggested, at least for the purposes of our discussion. So now that's my official view: mental states and activities are immaterial or nonphysical properties of the brain that influence and are influenced by the physical properties of the brain.

COHEN: Philosophers have a name for that position—it's "property dualism." Descartes was a *substance* dualist: there are two basic kinds of *things*, minds and bodies. Property dualists think there is just one kind of thing: brains *are* minds. But they are minds in virtue of their nonphysical properties. Property dualism is becoming a pretty respectable view these days.

MILLER: Well, then maybe Gretchen and I can agree to be a property dualists.

WEIROB: That would be nice. But I don't think there are any very good arguments for property dualism.

It's a bit more palatable than substance dualism, I'll give you that. And I'll admit, for the sake of argument, that interaction between physical and nonphysical properites of the same thing is more plausible than causal interaction between material bodies and immaterial minds—although I have my doubts about that. Even assuming that, I don't think I want to accept property dualism.

MILLER: Well, it was worth a try.

COHEN: There is another problem for you, Sam. I don't think property dualists think their view alone provides a reason for belief in anything like immortal souls. They think there are just material objects, but some of them, like the brain, have two kinds of properties. Experiences and thoughts do occur *in* the brain, even though they are not physical properties *of* the brain. So it's at least not obvious that these mental properties could continue to exist on their own, when the brain that has them has returned to dust and ashes. So, property dualism doesn't seem to lead to immortal minds or souls, at least not in any obvious way. Sorry, Sam.

MILLER: That's disappointing. But it would still be a relief to know that when I have experiences, when I consciously think and reason, or when I am in the midst of a difficult moral decision, it's not just a totally material brain at work in a mechanical way, like a computer inside my head. I really think there is more to me than that. If I can't be an immaterial substance, I at least want to have *some* properties of the sort that rocks and robots don't have.

So what exactly do you have against property dualism, Gretchen?

WEIROB: Let's reconstruct Ewing's experiment to see if I should be convinced. I'll be the materialist. You guys outfit me with some version of Herbert Feigl's* auto-cerebroscope....

MILLER: Auto-cerebroscope...?

COHEN: If I remember my Feigl, that's a device that allows one to examine his own brain visually, at the same time he is having experiences. Kind of like a miscroscope in one's own brain, hooked up to a TV set outside the brain.

WEIROB: That's it. The kind of auto-cerebroscope I have in mind is like the submarine in *Fantastic Voyage*, but without Arthur and Raquel. We control it from the outside. I can send it to any part of my brain to see what is going on there.

MILLER: Okay, so you grasp the red-hot poker. In spite of the incredible pain, you remain focused on philosopical issues. Maybe you release the poker, the pain abates, then you grab it again. You send the submarine to different parts of your brain until you find a spot, or spots, where there is a difference in brain activity. You examine these spots closely. You don't see anything that resembles the experience you are having.

WEIROB: That's the idea....

MILLER: This seems like a rather picturesque way of making Ewing's point, or Leibniz'. You won't see an experience. Or, since I am now a property dualist, maybe I should say that you'll see the event that is an experience, but you won't see the properties that make it an experience. But you can see all the physical properties. So the properties we are aware of when we have experiences aren't physical. Well done. You've done a great job destroying your own position.

WEIROB: But have I? I'm not so sure. We need to distinguish between materialism and physicalism. Materialism is an eighteenth-century view. Take an ordinary material object, like a rock. What Locke* would call its "primary qualities" are size, shape, motion, position, distance from other objects, solidity, things like that. Materialism is the view that that's all the properties anything has, including us and our brains.

COHEN: But of course we now know that's not right. . . .

WEIROB: Modern science recognizes all sort of other properties that are needed to explain what goes on at the microscopic and less than microscopic levels. The things that quantum physicists deal with don't just have primary qualities. Some of them don't really even have a position, as I understand it.

COHEN: I know there are quarks, some of which have "charm," and also leptons. But I don't really know what those things are. But they aren't material objects.

WEIROB: My point is that all I can see, even with my auto-cerebroscope, are material properties. I can't see what's going on at the quantum level. I can't see all of the *physical* properties. When we do our thought experiment—when you imagine the three of us looking at the screen of the auto-cerebroscope as I grab and release the poker—what are we looking for? Aren't we just looking for material properties, little bits of gray matter moving and changing with respect to their material properties and relations? But if experience-properties are physical properties that are not material properties, if they involve quarks being charming and the like, that won't show anything.

COHEN: That's not very convincing, Gretchen. None of *us* would know what to look for. But suppose you have three brilliant neuroscientists of the future conducting the experiment, with an incredible auto-cerebroscope that can focus on any part of the brain with any degree of precision. It can focus on things too small to see, even with a microscope, and somehow construct images to put on the screen of the auto-cerebroscope that represent the physical properties of these tiny events. The screen displays informaton about electrical phenomena. It can replay events in slow motion. These guys know the difference between the physical and the merely material, and they would know what to look for. But it still seems to me that there is *nothing* that would appear on the auto-cerebroscope that would resemble the feeling of pain, or even come close.

MILLER: Good point.

WEIROB: Dave, I admit that is a good point. But here's a more important consideration that I think gets at my main misgiving about the argument. Suppose Maude is the neuroscientist who holds the poker and has the pain. Then the argument is that Maude can see, via her auto-cerebroscope, everything that goes on in her brain, material or physical. And she feels her pain. She can't find anything going on in her brain that *looks* like her pain *feels*. But what does that show? She is basically comparing two experiences, the experience of feeling the pain and her visual experience of seeing her brain, or at least the image on the auto-cerebroscope. I agree that they are quite dissimilar experiences. But why should the experience of *having* a pain resemble the experience of *seeing* a pain?

Suppose Sam puts a bit of warm chocolate on his tongue while holding his mouth open and looking in the mirror. Then he can see and taste the same bit of chocolate. Two experiences that are quite different, but both are experiences *of* the same piece of chocolate. You wouldn't argue that what Sam is tasting is not what he is seeing, would you? I don't know that Ewing's argument, even the way you have spiced it up, is any better than that. I'll bet Maude would agree with me.

MILLER: I think I'm getting my mind, immaterial as it may be, around your way of looking at things. According to you, having a pain, or a nice taste sensation, is just being in a brain state—having certain kinds of physical activity in your brain. Ewing is right, that having that experience is quite unlike *seeing* it on an auto-cerebroscope or in any other way. But you are saying that doesn't prove his point. There is no reason to suppose that *being* in a brain state would be anything like *perceiving* that very same brain state.

WEIROB: Yes, that is exactly my view.

MILLER: It seems preposterous.

WEIROB: You see a contradiction? Or some other kind of incoherence in it?

MILLER: I can't say that I do. I need to think about it.

WEIROB: It's getting late. When we meet for lunch Wednesday, Sam can try to convince me to be a property dualist.

COHEN: Maybe I'll lend him a hand. I'm not sure whether or not I want to be a property dualist, but I'll help Sam with the arguments and then we'll see what Gretchen does to them.

MILLER: It's a deal.

WEDNESDAY

WEIROB: You can serve yourselves some fresh mushroom soup from the stove. Mushrooms are supposed to be good for clear thinking. Or is that avocados? Whatever. I baked some cookies, too. Dig in.

MILLER: I'm glad I'm not a zombie, so I'll enjoy the taste of your lunch.

WEIROB: Huh?

COHEN: Sam and I have been talking about zombies.

WEIROB: Zombies? Good Lord. Do you mean like zombies and vampires? We're going to do the philosophy of zombies and vampires? Perhaps discuss the fine conceptual points that determine whether something is a zombie or a vampire? I think zombies don't drink blood and vampires do. Is there more to be said? Give me a break!

MILLER: No, not *that* sort of zombies. We've been talking about *philosophical* zombies, an idea Dave and I came up with while discussing Ewing's experiment. We came up with two arguments for property dualism based on Ewing that we call the "the zombie argument" and "the knowledge argument."

WEIROB: Zombie argument! That's a bit eerie. And intriguing. Let's look at it first. Tell me more.

COHEN: Zombies are beings exactly like us—that is, exactly like us in every *physical* respect—but without experiences, without consciousness. If there *could* be such beings, if they are possible, if their existence does not involve a contradiction, that would show that experience and consciousness are not physical, wouldn't it? We would have to be property dualists and believe that key features of our minds are not just physical.

WEIROB: But there aren't any zombies. Your philosophical zombies are no more real than ordinary zombies. You are giving me science fiction. How can you make a philosophical point with science fiction?

COHEN: That's not quite fair, Gretchen. Philosophical views have consequences for what's *possible*. If a philosophical theory says something is possible that isn't possible, or something isn't possible that is possible, that's a good argument against it.

           You used this kind of argument once in class. You were talking about a Humean theory, that something is morally wrong if normal, well-brought-up people who think of someone else doing that thing have a feeling of aversion. You said that we can conceive of a world in which normal, well-brought-up people think torturing babies is just fine. But then it's possible that torturing babies is not morally wrong. But, you said, it is not *possible* that torturing babies is anything but morally wrong. So we must reject Hume's theory.

WEIROB: Did I say that was a definitive argument?

COHEN: You never say that anything is a definitive
           argument for anything. But you did say some-
           thing like this. Historical accounts have to be
           rejected if they entail that things didn't hap-
           pen that did happen. Scientific accounts have
           to be rejected if they say that things wouldn't
           happen in the actual world under particular
           circumstances, but they would. And philo-
           sophical accounts have to be rejected if they
           say that something is *not* logically and con-
           ceptually possible when it *is* logically and
           conceptually possible. That's just the principle
           we are using.

WEIROB: Okay. I admit the form of argument works.
           According to my view, physicalism, it is impos-
           sible for there to be beings that are physically
           just like us but have no experiences—what you
           are calling "zombies." But you are saying that
           it is possible for there to be such beings. So we
           must reject my theory.

           I admit, that's a good form of philosophical argu-
           ment. If I accept your premises, I must accept
           your conclusion. So I'll do my best not to accept
           your premises.

MILLER: Dave thinks there must be something wrong
           with the argument, but I think it's a great argu-
           ment. So we thought we would find out what
           you think—although I can already make a pretty
           good guess.

WEIROB: I think it's a fine argument, because it's an inter-
            esting argument. But I don't think it can be right.
            On that, I'm with Dave. In the end, I don't think
            we will find that zombies should convince us
            that our minds are not simply physical.

MILLER: Are you ready to explain why?

WEIROB: First of all, let's get a bit clearer by what we mean
            by "consciousness."

MILLER: Here we go again. I would've thought that con-
            sciousness is consciousness and that's that. But I
            suppose that's too simple.

WEIROB: We need to make sure we agree on what Ewing
            thought the materialist *would* have when she
            grasped the red-hot poker—and what your zom-
            bies *wouldn't* have, even if they grabbed it.
            Ewing is thinking about what Herbert Feigl calls
            "raw feels." Some philosophers call them "qua-
            lia." But I don't know whether it's pronounced
            "qu-AH-lia" or "qu-AI-lia." So I prefer "raw
            feels."

MILLER: I think "raw feels" sounds kind of sleazy. Why
            don't we just call them experiences?

WEIROB: Fine with me. The main point is, as Thomas
            Nagel* puts it, it's *like* something to have a pain,
            or see a tree, or think about whether to get out of
            bed. That's the raw feel—I mean the experience.
            Nagel says that bats must have experiences when
            they fly around guided by sonar. But that's a kind
            of experience humans don't have, and so we

can't know what it's like to be a bat. Even if we dissect a bat, we won't know. But we know what it's *like* to feel pain and how that is different than what it's *like* to taste a chocolate chip cookie. It doesn't *seem* like this is just a difference in which neurons are firing in my brain. People know a lot about the experiences they are having, while knowing next to nothing about what the neurons in their brains are doing.

MILLER: Okay, so far so good. I have experiences, and you're at least admitting that having an experience doesn't seem like just having various chemical and electrical things and subatomic stuff happening in one's brain. So what else might we mean by "consciousness"?

WEIROB: We naturally take humans to be the paradigms of consciousness. But there is a lot more to a human mind than just experiences. We have reason, or at least most of us have some reasoning abilities. We have self-consciousness. As Locke says, a person is aware of itself, as itself, in different times and places. And we have some kinds of higher-order consciousness. When Ewing's materialist grabs the red-hot poker, she will feel a pain, but she will also be aware she is feeling the pain. And if she is in a philosophical mood, she will have the pain, be aware of having the pain, and also be aware of being aware of having the pain. And so on. That's what human consciousness involves.

MILLER: Of course. What's the point?

WEIROB: I assume you will admit that dogs and frogs and perhaps even worms have pains and pleasures, and that it is like something for a dog to see or smell or hear things.

MILLER: Sure.

WEIROB: Well, I think so, too. But it's not obvious that they have much if any of the other things characteristic of human consciousness.

COHEN: If dogs aren't self-consciousness, does that mean your dog doesn't know who she is? She certainly seems to. When she's hungry, she doesn't seem to have any doubts about who is hungry. When she buries a bone, in order to dig it up and chew on it the next day when it is a little more interesting, isn't she making plans for her own future—sort of?

WEIROB: Hey look, I love my dog Penelope. I think she's great. She deals with life better than most people I know. And I'm sure that she knows who she is, in *some* sense. When she feels hungry, she makes sure to get the food in her own mouth. But I doubt very much it's anywhere near as complicated and layered as human self-consciousness. And I would be even more certain of the point if I had a pet frog or a pet worm. We each have a conception of ourselves as one human among others, with a long past and hopefully a long future. We think about ourselves, criticize ourselves, try to improve ourselves, and the like.

MILLER: Penelope is a very cute dog, but why are we discussing dogs?

WEIROB: I'm just trying to nail down the point that it's expe-
            riences we are worried about. Consciousness, in
            the sense of having experiences, may be *nec-
            essary* for all the complicated things involved
            in human consciousness. But it doesn't seem
            sufficient.

COHEN: I think I get your point. In the sense of relevant
            sense of "consciousness" a person who is asleep
            and dreaming is conscious. A senile person who
            no longer seems to be conscious of who they are
            or where they are or much of anything else is still
            conscious in this sense. Anything that has experi-
            ences is conscious.

WEIROB: Here's another way of making the point.
            Computers can do a lot of things, and every year
            they are able to do more and more things. We
            can imagine robots made to look like humans
            that we could talk to in the way we talk to other
            humans. It seems they can do, or soon will be
            able to do, lots of things that we consider part
            of human consciousness. They have sensors to
            determine what the world around them is like.
            They can compute, analyze information, and
            make inferences—the things we regard as think-
            ing in humans.

COHEN: Well, some philosophers, like John Searle*,
            would say that robots can't even do that. They
            can't compute, analyze, make inferences, or do
            anything that requires understanding. They do
            things that *simulate* those human activities, and
            that makes it convenient to use the same words
            we use for humans to describe what they are

doing. People in artificial intelligence want to say they have made computers that understand language, think, and reason. But they are exaggerating their accomplishments, impressive as they are. Philosophically speaking at least, we shouldn't use those words.

WEIROB: Good point, Dave. Maybe we can talk about Searle and artificial intelligence on another occasion. But for now, let's go along with the AI folk and say robots can think, reason, and understand, and can do all of those things in some reasonable sense. My point is that, even so, there still seems to be a big question: Would such robots, with computers for brains, really *experience* anything? When we put this as, "Would intelligent robots be *conscious?*" we're using "consciousness" in the way I'm getting at.

COHEN: So our zombies are sort of like robots, if we assume that robots *don't* have experiences. Now when you look inside a robot, you don't find anything like a human brain, but instead a computer or computers. They are silicon-based, not carbon-based. Perhaps that's a good reason to at least doubt that they have experiences. When you look inside a zombie, however, you find a human brain. Even so, Sam and I are suggesting that they don't have experiences. One might want to say that they compute and reason and plan and all of those things—we say those things about computers. But they don't have experiences, and so, in the sense we are using the word, they are not conscious.

MILLER: Great, we understand, so let's get on with it. If the pain Ewing's materialist feels when she grabs the red-hot poker involves nonphysical properties, I win. If there could be zombies with brains just like ours but no experiences, I win. If there could be zombie dogs just like Penelope, or zombie frogs just like the ones I hear croaking at night, I win.

COHEN: And I guess if we have a robot that has sensors and a great computer brain, seems to be aware of its surroundings, makes complicated plans, and writes a moving robot autobiography, it still wouldn't be *conscious* unless, in addition to all of that, it had experiences.

WEIROB: Right.

MILLER: Yes, right, right, agreed. Are we done with distinctions and terminology? Can we start discussing the zombie argument?

WEIROB: Okay. Let's look at the the argument. Explain it to me again.

MILLER: I'll let you do the honors, Dave.

COHEN: It's pretty simple. Consider an imaginary but possible world that is physically indiscernible from ours. "Indiscernible" here doesn't merely mean *looks the same,* but *is* exactly similar. But in this world, the zombie counterparts of humans have no experiences. It's not *like anything* to be a zombie. Their minds are blank. They don't have any *raw feels.* Excuse me, *experiences.* We say that computers "think" and robots "perceive" things. So we could say the same about zombies, if we wanted to. But, for them, it's not *like anything* to "think" and "perceive." No experiences are involved.

WEIROB: Suppose I succeed in imagining such a world, and admit that it is possible. What follows from that?

COHEN: Every physical event that happens in our world happens in the zombie world, too. But there are no experiences.

WEIROB: And . . . ?

COHEN: Since all the physical events are there, but the experiences aren't, experiences are not physical events. If the physical events and the physical properties of the brains are all there, but the experiences aren't, then experiences must not be physical properties. They may be properties of brains, but they have to be nonphysical properties, or they couldn't be missing in the zombie world. That's the argument.

WEIROB: Well, as I said, that is an interesting argument. An intriguing argument, even.

MILLER: How about a *convincing* argument.

WEIROB: I think I see a problem. Since your zombie world is physically indiscernible from the real one, there are three of these zombies sitting around eating lunch in a house just like this one. Words come out of their mouths—utterances are surely physical events—the same words that are coming out of our mouths as ours. But they aren't thinking. Right?

COHEN: They may be thinking the way computers think. But there is nothing going on inside the way there is when we think. When we think, it's *like* something. What it's like to think is much different than what it's like to eat a chocolate chip cookie, or have a toothache or Ewing's throb of intense pain. As experiences go, it's a bit subtle. Hume would say that what happens when we think and imagine and the like is less "lively and vivacious" than what happens when we perceive. But still it's like something to think.

MILLER: Well put, Dave. Ready to concede and become a dualist, Gretchen?

WEIROB: Well, maybe not quite yet. I need to know a little bit more about what it means for a world to be physically indiscernible from ours.

MILLER: How is that a problem? For every physical event that occurs in our world, the actual world, one exactly like it occurs in the zombie world. But that's all the events there are in the zombie world. So, as far as brains go and all other physical things, and all their physical properties are concerned, it's exactly similar. The only difference between the zombie world and the real one is the missing experiences. Is that clear enough for you?

WEIROB: Well, actually, no. I'm still not quite clear about what is going on in the zombie world. Let's try a couple of examples, to make sure I understand.

MILLER: Fine.

WEIROB: Dave, you just took a spoonful of the mushroom soup I made. How was it?

COHEN: Delicious, Gretchen. You are a great cook. Thanks for making lunch.

WEIROB: Now you said it was delicious. You made the sound, "delicious." That was a physical event, right? And a different physical event than if you had said, "Not the worst I've ever tasted," or "Completely foul."

COHEN: Quite right.

WEIROB: Now, assuming you are being truthful, is it fair to say that your response was due, at least in part, to how the soup tasted to you? That is, to what *experience* you had when you ate it?

COHEN: I was being truthful. I said it was delicious because of its taste—that is, because of the experience I had when I put it in my mouth and swished it around and swallowed it.

WEIROB: So you are saying that the cause, or at least part of the cause, for the physical event of saying "delicious" was the experience you had when you ate the soup?

COHEN: I think I see where you are going. But yes, part of the cause of my saying "delicious" is how it tasted, the experience I had.

WEIROB: Of course there was a lot more involved. You were responding to a question I asked. Your tongue and mouth muscles were all working. You are disposed to tell the truth. All sorts of things. But we can say, can't we, that the experience was a *necessary part* of the totality of conditions that were sufficient for you to say "delicious."

MILLER: Slow down, you're losing me.

COHEN: A sufficient condition for something to occur is a condition—usually a complex condition or set of conditions—that is enough to bring about the occurrence.

MILLER: Yes, I understand that.

COHEN: A necessary condition for something to occur is a condition without which the event wouldn't happen.

MILLER: I understand that, too. But when Gretchen talks about a necessary part of a sufficient condition, I get a little lost.

COHEN: She's getting at the point that what we usually call the "cause" of an event isn't usually, as one might think, *all* of the conditons that are necessary and sufficient for the event to happen.

Let's take another example. Suppose a wheel fell off a boxcar while the heavily loaded train it was part of was going around a curve. The boxcar leaves the rails, and then the whole train goes off the rails.

MILLER: It happens from time to time, even on the Rock Island Line.

COHEN: We'd say the wheel falling off the boxcar was the cause of the derailment. But the wheel falling off wasn't a *sufficient* condition for the derailment. If the train hadn't been moving it wouldn't have derailed. Perhaps if it hadn't been going around a curve, it wouldn't have derailed. Perhaps if it had been more lightly loaded, or going a lot slower, it wouldn't have derailed.

MILLER: I see. The wheel falling off all by itself was not sufficient for the derailment. It was the wheel falling off, *together* with the train going a fair speed, and going around a curve, and being fully loaded, that was sufficient.

COHEN: Right. Now notice that the wheel falling off isn't a *necessary* condition for the derailment either.

MILLER: Well, it was as I understood the example. I assumed that the train could have made it around the curve without derailing had the wheel not fallen off.

COHEN: Quite right. But the train could have derailed due to a different set of conditions. Perhaps someone had removed a rail. Or set off a bomb just as the train passed over it. The sufficient condition for the derailment would be different, and not involve the wheel falling off.

MILLER: Okay, it's not necessary, in an unconditional sense. But *given* the way the derailment happened, if you leave everything the same, and the wheel doesn't fall off, it doesn't derail. So it's necessary in that way.

COHEN: Exactly. And that's what Gretchen means by "a necessary part of a sufficient condition." The sufficient condition is the whole combination of things—going around a curve, heavily loaded, moving at a fair rate of speed. If you take away one of them, no derailment. So, they are each necessary parts of the sufficient condition that actually led to the derailment. At least, that's what I think she meant.

WEIROB: You've got it just right, Dave. Well explained. By the way, we philosophers have a term for this. We call things like the wheel falling off an "INUS condition."

MILLER: Huh?

WEIROB: That's short for an *i*nsufficient but *n*ecessary part of an *u*nnecessary but *s*ufficient condition. The actual sufficient condition—speed, curve, and missing wheel—isn't the only way the derailment could have occurred. So it's not a necessary condition of the derailment. It's an *u*nnecessary but *s*ufficient condition.

MILLER: I get it. The wheel falling off, as Dave pointed out, is *insufficient* by itself for the derailment—the train might have been going slow on a straight stretch of track. But it is a *necessary* part of the actual sufficient condition. So it's an INUS condition. Great, a new addition to my philosophical vocabulary.

COHEN: The idea comes from Mackie*, right?

WEIROB: Exactly. Brilliant fellow, Mackie.

COHEN: Mackie's point was that in a case like the train derailment, we would ordinarily say the wheel falling off *caused* the derailment. What we ordinarily call "causes" of an event are usually not *total* causes—not the whole complex of conditions that suffices for the event, but INUS conditions.

MILLER: This is all quite fascinating, I guess. But can we get back to the zombie argument now? Does anyone remember where we were?

WEIROB: I was getting Dave to admit that the experience he had, when he slurped up his soup, was an INUS condition for the physical event of his producing the sound "delicious."

COHEN: I never denied it. And I wasn't slurping. But, aside from that, that's where we were.

WEIROB: So then the experience Dave had, the pleasant experience of tasting perfectly concocted mushroom soup, was a cause, in the INUS sense, of his saying "delicious."

MILLER: Okay, okay. We grant you that. Get on with it.

WEIROB: Patience, Sam. My point is that in the zombie
            world, that pleasant experience doesn't occur.
            But, since the zombie world is physically indis-
            cernible from ours, in that world the physical
            event of zombie-Dave producing the sound
            "delicious" occurs, just as it does in the real
            world.

MILLER: Of course.

WEIROB: But *why* does it occur? If we remove the cause,
            or an essential part of the cause, don't we have
            to remove the effect, too?

MILLER: Well, it just happens.

WEIROB: But if he didn't have the pleasant experience,
            what accounts for his saying "delicious" rather
            than "foul" or something else? Or nothing?

MILLER: I don't see a contradiction there. You haven't
            shown that the zombie world isn't possible.

WEIROB: But if *nothing* causes him to say one thing rather
            than another, doesn't that mean that the zombie
            world isn't physically indiscernible? If it's physi-
            cally indiscernible, shouldn't the *same* physical
            events have the *same* causes in the zombie world
            that they do in the real world?

MILLER: Maybe the cause is the same, and it is purely
            physical in both worlds. It just *seems* to us that
            experiences cause physical events. Maybe the

zombie world shows that Dave's experience wasn't just an INUS condition even in the real world—it just seemed like it was.

WEIROB: So you are willing to embrace *epiphenomenalism*?

MILLER: Geez, more terminology. Embrace epi-whatism?

COHEN: Epiphenomenalism. In general, an epiphenomenon is an event that is caused, but that doesn't have any further effects, or at least none that are of interest. In philosophy, epiphenomenalism is the doctrine that experiences are just epiphenomena. That is, they have physical causes, but no physical effects.

WEIROB: Epiphenomenalism is a way of accommodating three things that seem plausible, at least to some people. First, property dualism. Experiences are nonphysical brain events. Second, physical events in our brains determine which experiences we have. Third, the physical world is a closed system. That means that physical events have only physical causes. That doesn't prevent them from having nonphysical effects. That's an assumption that has guided a lot of science for centuries.

COHEN: The epiphenomenalist picture goes like this. The soup being in my mouth, and its chemistry and the way my tastebuds work, caused a chain of physical events, including my saying "delicious." That physical process *also* caused me to have an experience. But, contrary to how it seemed to me, that experience *wasn't* the cause, or even part of the cause, of my saying "delicious." Experiences don't cause physical events, so the assumption that the physical world is "closed" is safe, even if physical events cause experiences. The experience wasn't an INUS condition, as it seemed, but merely an epiphenomenon. So, when we leave experiences out of the zombie world, we aren't leaving out any causes of physical events. So we don't have to leave out any effects.

MILLER: Well, if I understand what you two are saying, given epiphenomenalism, the zombie world *can* be physically indiscernible from the actual world. So the zombie world makes sense. I don't see how Gretchen can claim that the failure of physical events to cause nonphysical events constitutes a *physical* difference.

WEIROB: I'll agree to that. I agree that *if* we accept epiphenomenalism, then the zombie world can be physically indiscernible from the actual world.

MILLER: So, don't I win?

WEIROB: Not if you're trying to convince me of dualism. You'd first have to convince me of epiphenomenalism. The zombie argument works only if we add epiphenomenalism as an extra premise. And I don't accept the extra premise. Epiphenomenalism seems crazy to me.

MILLER: Crazy? That's kind of harsh.

WEIROB: Okay, I retract "crazy." I'll just say extremely implausible and unattractive.

MILLER: Right this minute it seems plausible and attrac-
             tive to me.

COHEN: Look, Sam, do you really want to accept that the
             pains and joys we experience, the experiences
             we have when we see or feel or taste something,
             have no effect on what we do? No effect on the
             physical actions we perform—movements of our
             limbs of our tongues and vocal chords, as when I
             said "delicious"? Isn't that a high price to pay for
             accepting the zombie argument?

MILLER: When you put it that way, I must admit I'm not
             too enthusiastic about accepting epiphenom-
             enalism. But isn't there some evidence for it?

WEIROB: Such as?

MILLER: Suppose after Gretchen took the soup off the
             electric burner, while the coil was still red hot, I
             put my hand on it.

COHEN: Back to Ewing?

MILLER: But I'm making a different point. I would feel
             pain, and I would remove my hand from the
             burner very quickly. But is it so clear that the
             pain *causes* my hand to move? Suppose some
             physiologist does a careful study and shows
             that the movement of my hand actually begins
             a nanosecond or two *before* I feel that pain.
             I think I've read about studies along these
             lines. The physiologist concludes that the pain
             doesn't cause the movement, but that the effect
             of the heat on my hand causes both the pain

and the movement, in such a way that it *seems* that the pain caused the movement. I don't see anything to show that he wouldn't be right. My pain would be an epiphenomenon, in your terminology.

WEIROB: Okay, I'll grant you that. But suppose that when you touched the burner you were a small child. You didn't know why the burner was red. You put your hand on it. You felt pain and removed your hand. We grant that pain doesn't cause the removal of your hand. But won't it have *other* physical effects? Won't you be much less likely to put your hand on a red burner in the future? Suppose when Dave ate the soup, the taste he experienced was foul. Wouldn't he be much less likely to take another spoonful of the soup? Even if we grant that experiences don't have all the physical effects we think they do, don't we have to suppose that they have *some* effects on our physical brain that affects our future physical behavior?

MILLER: That's a good point, I admit. It seems like having one experience rather than another sometimes affects future behavior. It's hard to see why that would happen if the experience doesn't affect the brain somehow. Hard, but not impossible. The physical events that cause the pain could also cause a physical state that prevents us from doing the same thing again.

COHEN: But think about it, Sam. Insofar as having a profound effect on what we think being a human being amounts to, wouldn't the truth of epiphenomenalism be an even *bigger* blow than the truth of physicalism? We see ourselves as beings that do what we do because of the experiences we have—not everything we do, but a lot of it. If epiphenomenalism is true, this is just a big illusion. I'm not finishing this soup because it tasted so good. Gretchen isn't talking to us because she enjoys talking philosophy. You don't go to the beach on summer days because of how good it feels to lie in the sun. And so on. It seems to me a very dismal view of human life.

MILLER: Well, I guess I can't deny that. So where does that leave us?

WEIROB: I think it leaves us here. If epiphenomenalism is true, then the zombie world is possible. The absence of experiences doesn't imply that there is a physical difference between it and the real world. But if you don't accept epiphenomenalism, removing experiences removes some of the causes of physical events. So removing the experiences from the world will make it physically different. All the things for which experiences are INUS conditions won't happen.

So maybe the zombie argument should persuade epiphenomenalists to become dualists. But it won't persuade me, because I'm not an epiphenomenalist. So I don't think you can remove experiences without removing their effects, which means that your zombie world will *not* be physically indiscernible from the real world.

MILLER: You've given me something to think about. But
              I'm not convinced. It's getting late. I need to meet
              with some parishioners over at the church. We
              need to continue with epiphenomenalism when
              we meet Friday. By then I hope to have figured
              out some sort of response. Or maybe Dave will.

COHEN: And remember, Sam, we've still got our knowl-
              edge argument to discuss. So I'll see you both
              Friday? Can we count on you for lunch again,
              Gretchen?

WEIROB: I think so. I'm in all the right mental states to
              make another nice meal. But if epiphenomenal-
              ism is true, who knows what will happen?

MILLER: Ha, ha. So long.

FRIDAY

WEIROB: Come in. French onion soup today.

I'm eager to hear what you have to say, Sam. Are you still an epiphenomenalist? Or have you given up on the zombie argument?

MILLER: Actually, neither. I've decided I don't want to be an epiphenomenalist. I admit that in the actual world, experiences do causally affect the physical world. My experiences affect my brain, and my bodily movements, and through them, all sorts of things.

WEIROB: But you still haven't given up on the zombie argument?

MILLER: No, I've been thinking about it, and now I think you hoodwinked us Wednesday.

WEIROB: How so?

MILLER: You convinced us that if we are not epiphenomenalists, then we need to suppose that experiences are INUS conditions for physical events. You seduced us into saying "is an INUS condition for" instead of "causes." But causes *don't* need to be INUS conditions.

COHEN: Tell me more.

49

MILLER: Take your derailed train example. The wheel coming off the freight car caused the derailment. But suppose that one of the rails the train was approaching was loose. The passage of the train, up to the freight car, loosened it more. At the very second the wheel falls off, or perhaps a nano-second later, the rail falls off the ties. The wheel falling off is a cause of the train derailing. But it's *not* a necessary condition. The train would have fallen off the tracks, even if the wheel hadn't fallen off the boxcar.

WEIROB: Your point is that the zombie argument could go off the rails for many different reasons?

MILLER: Ha ha. No my point is that I can claim that experiences are like that. In the real world, they cause all sort of things. In the zombie world, something *else* causes those things, something that was *redundant* in the real world. So the zombie world can be just like ours physically, even though there are no experiences. If that's what the zombie world is like, I don't have to be an epiphenomenalist and deny that in the real world experiences cause physical changes. It's just that in the zombie world, something else causes them, something that happens in the real world but doesn't do the causing here.

COHEN: Interesting. I think there are three scenarios here that we need to distinguish, however.

MILLER: Say more.

COHEN: First, there is a case that I don't think you had in mind, where the combination of the wheel falling off and the rail tumbling off the ties causes the derailment. Neither alone would have sufficed. They are both INUS conditions.

MILLER: You're right. That's not what I had in mind.

COHEN: I just mention it to get it out of the way. Then there are two somewhat different cases. Philosophers call them "preemption" and "overdetermination."

MILLER: Oh good, more terminology. You guys may not teach me anything about experiences, but you are definitely increasing my vocabulary. But I'm interrupting—go on, Dave....

COHEN: In both cases, we assume that the wheel falling off would have caused the derailment, even if the rail had stayed in place. And the rail toppling off the ties would have caused the derailment, even if the wheel hadn't fallen off the freight car.

MILLER: That's what I had in mind.

COHEN: If the wheel falls off first—even a nanosecond before, as you put it—then it is *the* cause. The rail toppling was *preempted* as a cause; it didn't have a chance to cause the derailment, because the wheel falling off the boxcar already had. On the other hand, if they happen at the same time—the rail tumbles just as the wheel falls—we have *overdetermination*. Two causes, each of which was enough even without the other.

MILLER: I see the difference. What I had in mind was what you call "preemption," I think, although maybe overdetermination would work as well.

So, Gretchen, ready to be a property dualist?

WEIROB: Well, not yet. Your idea is that in the zombie world, physical states cause physical effects that they would cause in the real world, if experiences did not preempt them. But in the real world, experiences *are* causes. So you don't have to be an epiphenomenalist.

By the way, just for the record, Mackie eventually changed "necessary" to "nonredundant" in the definition of INUS condition, to take care of preemption.

MILLER: Well, good for him. But let's not think about definitions. Think about my point. You had it exactly right. So I have an experience doing the job we think they do in the actual world; I don't need to be an epiphenomenalist. But the same things happen without them, in the physically indiscernible zombie world, because of the things that would have caused them in the actual world, had the experiences not beat them to it. Don't you admit that this is perfectly coherent?

WEIROB: Yes, I do. And I admit that I was wrong in thinking that you had to be an epiphenomenalist to be convinced by the zombie argument.

MILLER: So are you ready to accept the argument and be a dualist?

WEIROB: Not at all.

MILLER: Why not?

WEIROB: You aren't now committed to epiphenomenal-
           ism. I'll grant you that. Indeed, I congratulate
           you. Very clever. But now you seem to be com-
           mitted to the view that every time an experience
           causes anything physical, in the *real* world, it's
           a case of preemption. Or of overdetermination.
           If that weren't true of the real world, the same
           things wouldn't happen in the zombie world.
           You think that although experiences cause things
           in the real world, they aren't really *necessary* for
           their effects. I suppose we could call your view
           "unnecessaryism."

COHEN: Unnecessaryism seems a bit more palatable than
           epiphenomenalism. One can continue to sup-
           pose that things happen because of our feelings
           and thoughts, even though they would have hap-
           pened without them. But it seems a rather strange
           view.

WEIROB: Strange, yes, but more importantly, obviously
           false. Or, at the very least, a view for which there
           is no evidence.

MILLER: Why do you say that?

WEIROB: I certainly accept that cases of preemption can
           occur. Wednesday Dave said "delicious" when I
           asked him how the soup tasted. We all admitted
           that the pleasant taste caused the physical event
           of his saying that.

MILLER: Agreed.

WEIROB: Now just suppose that, for some reason we don't
              need to go into, someone else very much wanted
              Dave to tell me that the soup was delicious. A
              very determined and violent person. He showed
              Dave a gun, and said that if he didn't tell me that,
              he would shoot him.

COHEN: Maybe he gave you the recipe, and you said you
              would give him $100 if I liked it, and he is very
              desperate for money.

WEIROB: If you insist on a backstory, that will do.

MILLER: Get to the point.

WEIROB: So these are the facts. Dave fully intends to
              say "delicious," even before tasting the soup,
              because he doesn't want to be shot.

COHEN: I certainly did. Or would have. And wouldn't.
              Like to be shot, that is.

WEIROB: But in fact the soup is so good that he imme-
              diately and spontaneously says "delicious,"
              simply because it tasted so good. If it hadn't
              tasted good, he would have said it anyway.
              So, the pleasant taste preempted the fear
              of getting shot, as far as causing him to say
              "delicious."

MILLER: That's a good case. Nothing mysterious about
              preemption. That seems to help my cause.

WEIROB: I grant that preemption is not all that mysterious, and probably does occur. But rarely. Notice how odd and unusual this case is. It's interesting precisely because it's unusual. A huge coincidence. That sort of thing simply doesn't happen all that often. But you are asking me to accept that *every time* an experience causes something in the real world, it is a case of preemption. That may be less preposterous than epiphenomenalism, but it's surely still wildly implausible.

COHEN: On Sam's view, it's a little hard to explain anesthetics. When the dentist gives me novocaine, it blocks the pain. But it also keeps me from shouting and writhing in agony and calling her names. If the pain were preempting other causes of my doing those things, I would continue to do them even after the shot of novocaine. I would even say, "Stop, doctor, it hurts like crazy." Sam could say that the novocaine does more than block the pain, I guess. Perhaps it also somehow eliminates the preempted states, too. But it certainly doesn't seem that we ordinarily think of experiences as unnecessary for their effects.

WEIROB: We don't think that every time a sensation causes a physical reaction there is some cause "waiting in the wings," so to speak, that gets preempted.

COHEN: So, Sam, do you really want to adopt unnecessaryism? Aside from the ugly name Gretchen gave it, it doesn't seem all that plausible.

MILLER: Well, I guess not. It seemed like a good idea a minute ago. Now it seems like a rather large and ad hoc assumption, even to save the zombie argument. And perhaps I don't need it.

WEIROB: You've got another idea?

MILLER: Yes. Something Dave said about the pain in the dentist's chair made me remember the second argument Dave and I thought up the other day.

COHEN: Our *knowledge* argument. It's really a variation on Ewing's original argument, I think. We think your reply to Ewing missed an important point.

WEIROB: But I argued, very cogently as I remember it, that even if the experience of pain were a brain process, it would not follow that having the experience—that is, *having* the process occur in your brain—should be anything like *seeing* the process occur in your brain via an autocerebroscope.

COHEN: Yes, you replied very cogently. And we accept your point. But we think perhaps Ewing's example brings out another gap that provides a better argument. I've been reading some more Feigl, and we want to throw in a new wrinkle that he suggests.

WEIROB: You are going to make the piece of iron even hotter? Perhaps you are going to make the physicalist pick up the bar of iron with her toes? I can't wait.

COHEN: No, those aren't quite what we have in mind. Feigl notes that a martian who was incapable of seeing color might nevertheless know all about how color vision works in humans. Thomas Nagel also supposed that martians are a superintelligent species of bats who wonder what it's like to be human, just as we humans can wonder what it's like to be a bat. Suppose these martians, whatever they are like, kidnapped some earthlings on a secret visit to our planet, and intensely studied how these earthlings worked. If color-vision experiences are all just brain processes, it seems the martians could have learned all about them.

WEIROB: So far, this is plausible, assuming they applied their superior martian intelligence to the problem. So some completely color-blind martian scientist knows how human brains work, and everything about how color vision works in particular?

COHEN: Exactly. Everyone knows how bright those martians are.

But if our martian scientist can't experience color, it seems he *couldn't really* know *everything* about color vision. The martian might know exactly what goes on in my brain when I see red. I might be very ignorant about such things—as indeed I am. Still, it seems I would know *what it is like* to see red or orange or blue, and he would not.

MILLER: So, there is a *knowledge* gap, rather than an *experience* gap. There is a bit of knowledge that the martian lacks—what it is like to see red. But he knows everything about what physical stuff goes on in the brain when a human sees red. So it seems that there is more to be known than just the physical facts. There must be *non*physical facts about the experience of seeing red that one can only know by *having* the experience.

COHEN: Which is to say they must involve nonphysical properties. And so, we are led back to property dualism.

WEIROB: That's pretty interesting. Can't we get by without bringing in martians, though? A blind person or a deaf person could make the same point, right? We could imagine the person somehow regaining sight or hearing, and coming to have the relevant experiences and so coming to know what he couldn't know before—at least according to the argument.

COHEN: Good idea. Let's go back to my dentist. Call her Mildred. Mildred has observed a lot of patients with painful toothaches over the years, and has relieved a lot of their pain. But she has never herself had a toothache. She was raised in a town with natural flouride. Her parents were both dentists, and they insisted that she brush and floss three times a day. She never had a cavity. She was never in any other situation that would lead to a toothache. She has never *experienced* a toothache.

WEIROB: Okay, we've got a dentist who has never had a toothache. I suppose now she is going to have one, for the first time.

COHEN: Exactly, but not yet. First, after leaving dental school, she earns a Ph.D. in neuroscience. Her dissertation is on the neural basis of toothaches.

WEIROB: And then . . . ?

COHEN: Then, for the first time, she actually *has* a full-blown toothache. A bad one.

WEIROB: How does that come about?

COHEN: Well, it doesn't really matter. Let's suppose she accidentally bit down on a stone and broke one of her lower teeth. A premolar on the left side, if you want me to be specific. It breaks, and she is in the throes of a bad toothache.

WEIROB: So far, so sad.

COHEN: You will admit, won't you, that when this happens she *learns* something she didn't know before.

WEIROB: Not to bite down on rocks? She must have known that. I'm sure her parents told her to be careful about things like that.

MILLER: No, not that. C'mon, Gretchen, you are being annoying. I'm not as patient as Dave. She learns *what it is like* to have a toothache.

WEIROB: Sorry. I wanted to learn what it was like to be annoying. I'll try to do better. So, I assume Mildred has experienced other sorts of pain?

MILLER: Yes. But toothaches constitute a rather specific kind of pain, or range of pains. Toothaches are pretty different from headaches and sprains and cuts and bruises.

WEIROB: When she was writing her dissertation, I assume she dealt with a lot of people with toothaches. Maybe she chatted with them while hooking them up to a cerebroscope. Couldn't they just have *told her* what it was like to have a toothache?

MILLER: We can grant that she knew a lot *about* what it was like. She knows that toothaches have a very specific feel to them. They are different than headaches or backaches. Perhaps, based on conversation, she could go on for quite a while about what it's like to have a toothache, or specifically to have a broken premolar. But still, it seems to us that there is something that she would learn when she actually breaks her tooth and has a toothache. Don't you agree?

WEIROB: I think I may as well agree. Otherwise, you will drag me through a succession of blind scientists, deaf sound engineers who use meters and oscilloscopes, or even go back to Feigl's martians. So, I'll agree. The first time she actually has a toothache, there is something Mildred learns. She may have known everthing that could be known about the physical aspects of teeth and brains. She may have learned quite a lot about what it's like to have a toothache from talking to people who have them. But, I grant, there is a very central part of knowing what it's like to have a toothache that she didn't know until she had one. So she learned something. So what?

MILLER: If she learned something, then there must be a fact she did not know. But, by hypothesis, she knew all the physical facts involved in having a toothache. So the fact she learned must be a nonphysical fact. Nonphysical facts involve nonphysical properties. So experiences have nonphysical properties. These are their most central properties, *what it's like to have them.* The point is proven. Q.E.D.

COHEN: So, Gretchen, are you willing to concede that experiences are not physical? At least not wholly physical?

WEIROB: Maybe not quite yet. I admit this "knowledge argument" is interesting, a big improvement on Ewing's version. . . .

MILLER: I feel a "but" coming. . . .

WEIROB: . . . But I have a feeling that the problem here is with knowledge, and it doesn't show much about physicalism. At any rate, there is something I need you to clarify.

             You say that Mildred learns a new *fact.* Usually we identify facts with phrases like, "that so is so is such and such." For example, "It is a fact that Germany is part of Europe," or "It is a fact that water boils at 212 degrees." But you say that Mildred learns "what it is like to have a toothache." That doesn't sound to me like learning a *fact.*

MILLER: What else is there to learn, than facts?

WEIROB: That's sort of my point. There are other things to
            learn. We learn *how* to do things—how to ride
            a bicycle, for example. That doesn't seem to be
            a matter of learning facts. Maybe learning *what
            something is like* is more like that. So I just want
            to be clear. You do mean to be talking about
            learning a fact, right?

COHEN: I'll answer that. Yes, definitely. Mildred could
            use the fact language. Let's call Mildred's state
            "PTI" for "painful tooth injury." She could say, "I
            just learned that PTI feels like *this*." It's straight-
            forward. There is a certain aspect or quality that
            PTI has. She can refer to that aspect directly, with
            "this." She is in a position to refer to it that way,
            because she is directly aware of that aspect of
            PTI. So it seems like a perfectly proper fact.

WEIROB: Is this an aspect of PTI that only Mildred can
            refer to, and only when she is having it?

COHEN: No, not at all. Suppose, in order to contribute to
            philosophical understanding, Sam agrees to have
            his tooth injured in exactly the same way. . . .

MILLER: Fat chance.

COHEN: You don't actually have to do it.

MILLER: I knew that.

COHEN: At any rate, Sam's brain also goes into the PTI
            state, which we can verify with our cerebro-
            scope. He and Mildred are both in the PTI state.
            Can't Sam say, "Mildred just learned that PTI has

the property of feeling like *this*." He and Mildred both use "this" to refer to the "what it's like" aspect of the PTI state.

WEIROB: So we are talking about an objective fact here.

COHEN: We are assuming that the same brain states, at least in normal people in normal circum-stances, lead to the same nonphysical phenom-ena, the same feelings, the same "what it's like" phenomena.

MILLER: I think Mildred and I could refer to it later, too, when the pain was gone. We could still remem-ber what it was like to have a PTI.

WEIROB: Could you give that aspect of PTI a name? Maybe "molar-ouch"? Or assign an adjective to it, "molar-ouchy"? Sam might say to Mildred, "If I ever have a toothache again, I hope it's not a molar-ouchy one."

MILLER: I don't see why not.

WEIROB: Then couldn't I say this? "I know what it's like to have a PTI, even though I've never had the expe-rience. It's very molar-ouchy."

MILLER: That's just a trick. I can use a name without really knowing what it stands for. A mathematician tells me he is fascinated by complex numbers. I have no idea what a complex number is—beyond knowing that it's some kind of number a mathematician could be fascinated by. Still, I can say things like, "Complex numbers must be fascinating" and "I'll bet there is a book about complex numbers." Just because you can use "molar-ouchy" in a sentence doesn't mean you know what it's like to be in a molar-ouchy state. You can even learn things about it. I tell you that being in a molar-ouchy state is worse than having a sprained ankle. Then you can tell Dave that. It doesn't show that you know *what it is like* to be in a molar-ouchy state.

WEIROB: Your example brings up an interesting point. It's not like we don't recognize nonphysical properties and facts. The fact that 81 has 9 as its square root seems like a nonphysical fact, involving the nonphysical property, having 9 as a square root.

COHEN: Some philosophers think that such facts are reducible to facts about numerals, or facts about sets of physical objects.

WEIROB: Granted. But I don't know if any of them have come up with a convincing story. I'd love it if someone did. But the philosophy of mathematics is above my pay grade.

            My point is that those who think of mathematical facts as nonphysical get along just fine. They develop theories of these nonphysical facts involving nonphysical objects. They prove things. They apply what they have learned in the physical world, in science and engineering. There is a science of numbers.

MILLER: Fine. So what?

WEIROB: So this. Suppose you convince me that there are these nonphysical properties, like being molar-ouchy, that are aspects of brain states, in addition to their physical properties. Can I develop a science of these properties? Let me call them "qualic," with a long "a." Couldn't I study qualic properties in a systematic way and develop a theory called, say, qualic science? Of course, I don't mean that *I* could, but a properly funded brilliant person should be able to.

MILLER: It would be a pretty painful enterprise, if you wanted to develop the theory of the qualic properties of toothaches. You'd have to experience all kinds of toothaches, wouldn't you? Or this brilliant, well-funded person would have to.

WEIROB: He could get a huge grant and pay you and Dave to have more toothaches, and then ask you questions about your experiences. Smash molars on the other side of your mouths, and ask you to compare the molar-ouchy properties of the new injuries with the properties of the original ones. He could put a thumbscrew on Dave and tighten it until he said the pain he was experiencing was as bad as the toothache. Stuff like that.

MILLER: I think you are enjoying your thought experiment a little too much, Gretchen.

COHEN: I don't think the Human Subjects Committee would allow it.

MILLER: Probably not. But continue.

WEIROB: Let's further assume that property dualism becomes generally accepted, and qualic science thrives. Experiments are done. Theories are developed. Terms are introduced. Peer-reviewed journals are started. Grants are obtained. Chairs of qualic science are established. Okay so far?

MILLER: I'm not sure, but proceed.

WEIROB: You should like this story. Your view turns out to be right. Property dualism becomes part of science.

COHEN: I think I see what's coming.

WEIROB: Now Mildred's daughter, Debby, wants to pursue the same career path as her mother. She goes to dentistry school and learns all about teeth, just as Mildred did. Then she earns her Ph.D. in neuroscience. As part of that, she learns qualic science, which has been developed since her mother earned her degree. In particular, she learns how different kinds of pains differ and resemble one another in their nonphysical, qualic properties. There are, we may suppose, terms in qualic science for the different experiences *normally* associated with various kinds of damage or injuries to various teeth. There are various predicates and parameters—intensity, location, throbbing or not throbbing, ouchiness, etc.—associated with these various terms.

            Now Debby, like Mildred, is obsessively dedicated to the health of her teeth. She never had a damaged or injured tooth. Then one day Mildred tells her about the time she broke her tooth.

COHEN: And I suppose Debby tells her mother that she—Debby—knows just what that was like?

WEIROB: Sure, why not?

"Which tooth was it?" she asks.

"My left lower premolar."

"Had you been drinking or smoking weed, or anything like that?"

"No, everything was normal for me—sane and sober but with a broken tooth."

"Well, then, I know exactly what it was like. According to my *Qualic Science* text, since you are right-handed, a tooth injury like that has the qualic aspect TA-ABA. Ooh, that sounds very bad. But it would have been even worse if it had been your right lower premolar, instead of your left. Then it would have been a pure TA-AAA. That would have really throbbed."

So, do you agree with Debby, that she knew what it was like to have her mother's toothache?

MILLER: Of course not. She consults her book, and comes up with the right *label* for what it was like to have her mother's toothache. But Debby won't *really* know what it was like, until she breaks her own lower premolar. I suspect that's what her mother would have said.

COHEN: If you are right about that, Sam, we have a problem.

MILLER: Why is that?

COHEN: It looks like the same argument we used to show that experiences are *not* physical can be used to show that they can't be nonphysical either. Debby knows all the qualic, nonphysical properties involved in having damaged teeth. She knows exactly what *non*physical states someone like her mother with a broken left lower premolar was in. But, according to you, she still wouldn't know what it was like to have the experience her mother had until she had an experience of the same sort. So doesn't that show that experiences aren't *non*physical states, either?

MILLER: Oh dear.

WEIROB: That doesn't seem to be the conclusion to draw. It seems that if "what it's like to have a toothache" is a property of the experience of having a toothache, then it must be either a physical or a nonphysical property. But the same basic argument purports to show that it can't be either. So the right conclusion is that there is something wrong with the argument.

MILLER: Well, are you going to tell us what's wrong with the argument?

WEIROB: No. As I said, I think that it is really a problem about knowledge, and the nature of facts, not about property dualism. To understand what's wrong with this argument, we'll need another week of philosophizing-while-eating-lunch to talk about knowledge and facts. At least.

But, for now, I think I've shown that all your arguments that experiences can't be physical are no good. Or at any rate, not irresistable. My physicalist conscience is intact. Can I relax?

MILLER: Well, I haven't convinced you that experiences are nonphysical. I've run out of arguments. But I'm not convinced that they are physical. I guess that's the nature of philosophy.

By the way, did you just come up with that argument on the fly?

WEIROB: No, I remembered it from an article by a brilliant fellow named Paul Churchland*.

MILLER: Nice name, Churchland. Seems like he should have been a cleric. And a dualist. Sad.

COHEN: Well, friends, it's been a fun week. But classes begin again on Monday, and I've got an essay in history due then. So, gotta go. Thanks for the lunches and thanks for the philosophy, and I hope we get together again soon.

MILLER: I've got a sermon to write for Sunday. I've spent all week thinking about arguments against physicalism, but I doubt I can squeeze much of a sermon out of those ideas. So I'd better get a move on. So, thanks to both of you for a great week.

WEIROB: I suppose I should get busy on my lectures for Monday. But I look forward to the next time we can spend a whole week on one problem! It's been fun.

BIBLIOGRAPHY

Asterisks indicate key works by figures who are mentioned in the text.

*Berkeley, George. *Three Dialogues Between Hylas and Philonous* [1713]. Edited with an Introduction by Robert Merrihew Adams. Indianapolis: Hackett Publishing, 1979.

Block, Ned. "On a Confusion about a Function of Consciousness." *Behavioral and Brain Sciences* 18 (1995): 227–47. [An important article on different kinds of consciousness.]

Block, Ned, Owen Flanagan, and Güven Güzeldere, eds. *The Nature of Consciousness*. Cambridge: Bradford-MIT, 1997.

Chalmers, David. *The Conscious Mind*. New York: Oxford University Press, 1996. [Modern statement of the arguments for property dualism, putting forward both the zombie and knowledge arguments.]

*Churchland, Paul. "Knowing Qualia: A Reply to Jackson." Chap. 4 in *A Neurocomputational Perspective*. Cambridge: Bradford-MIT.

*Descartes, René. *Meditations on First Philosophy* [1641]. In René Descartes, *Discourse on Method and Meditations on First Philosophy*. Translated by Donald A. Cress. Indianapolis: Hackett Publishing, 1999.

*Descartes, René. *Discourse on Method* [1637]. In René Descartes, *Discourse on Method and Meditations on First Philosophy.* Translated by Donald A. Cress. Indianapolis: Hackett Publishing, 1999.

*Princess Elizabeth and René Descartes. *The Correspondence Between Princess Elizabeth of Bohemia and René Descartes* [1643–1649]. Edited and Translated by Lisa Shapiro. Chicago: University of Chicago Press, 2007.

*Ewing, A. C. *The Fundamental Questions of Philosophy.* New York: Collier Books, 1962.

*Feigl, Herbert. *The Mental and the Physical: The Essay and a Postscript.* Minneapolis: University of Minnesota Press, 1967. [This is a reprint that includes an added postscript of "The 'Mental' and the `Physical,'" in Herbert Feigl, Michael Scriven, and Grover Maxwell, *Minnesota Studies in the Philosophy of Science,* vol. II. Minneapolis: University of Minnesota Press, 1958.]

Gertler, Brie. "Review of Perry." *Notre Dame Philosophical Reviews* 5 (Jan. 2002). [Defense of zombie argument.]

Jackson, Frank. "What Mary Didn't Know." *The Journal of Philosophy* LXXXIII (1986): 291–95. [Classic statement of knowledge argument.]

*Leibniz, Gottfried. *Monadology* [1714]. In *G. W. Leibniz: Discourse on Metaphysics and Other Essays.* Translated by Daniel Garber and Roger Ariew. Indianapolis: Hackett Publishing, 1991.

*Locke, John. *An Essay Concerning Human Understanding* [1689]. Abridged and edited by Kenneth P. Winkler. Indianapolis: Hackett Publishing, 1996.

W. G. Lycan, ed. *Mind and Cognition: A Reader.* Oxford: Basil Blackwell, 1989.

*Mackie, J. L. "Causes and Conditions." *American Philosophical Quarterly* 12 (1965): 245–65.

Metzinger, Thomas, ed. *Conscious Experience.* Schöningh: Imprint Academic, 1995.

*Nagel, Thomas. "What Is It Like to Be a Bat?" *The Philosophical Review* 83 (1974): 435–50.

Nemirow, Laurence. "Physicalism and the Cognitive Role of Acquaintance." In W. G. Lycan, ed. *Mind and Cognition: A Reader.* Oxford: Basil Blackwell, 1989.

Nida-Rümelin, Martine. "What Mary Couldn't Know: Belief about Phenomenal States." In Thomas Metzinger, *Conscious Experience*, 218–41. Schöningh: Imprint Academic, 1995. [Against the knowledge argument.]

Perry, John. *Knowledge, Possibility and Consciousness.* Boston: MIT, 2001. [Defense of physicalism.]

Perry, John. "Return of the Zombies?" In Simone Gozzano and Christopher S. Hill, eds., *New Perspectives on Type Identity: The Mental and the Physical*, 251–63. Cambridge: Cambridge University Press, 2012. [Against the zombie argument.]

*Searle, John. "Minds, Brains and Programs." *Behavioral and Brain Sciences* 3 (1980): 417–57.

Skokowski, Paul. "I, Zombie." *Consciousness and Cognition* 11 (1) (2002): 1–9. [Against the zombie argument.]

GLOSSARY

Consciousness. In its ordinary use, "conscious" is close in meaning to "aware." To say someone is conscious implies that he or she is awake and aware of his or her surroundings; to say that someone is conscious of a particular pheonomenon is to say that he or she is aware of it, perceptually or in some other way. But in philosophy the term is used more broadly to mean having experiences, so that a person who is dreaming could be said to be conscious. This is the basic meaning of the term in the dialogue. There is also a wider use, for forms of intelligent activity, that shows awareness of various phenomena, as in "self-consciousness" and "moral consciousness."

Dualism. The terms "dualism" and "monism" are used in philosophy when there is a debate about whether one or two basic things, properties, principles, etc. are involved in the phenomenon under discussion. For example, a moral philosopher who thinks that empathy and reason both provide a basis for the difference between right and wrong actions might be called a dualist, in contrast with one who thinks reason alone does the job. In this dialogue, the debate is about *mind and body* dualism. Are there two basic kinds of things or properties in the world, mental and physical? Or is a mind just a special kind of physical thing, so there is only one basic kind?

Cartesian dualism is the view, put forward by René Descartes (1596–1650) in his *Meditations* and elsewhere, that a person's mind and body are two things, intimately connected through causation, but separated at death, when the mind (or soul) leaves the body. The mind and body are not only different things, but things of basically different kinds. Descartes believed that bodies and minds have different *essences*— that is, basic properties required for existence. Bodies are *extended*—that is, they take up space, and thus have shape, size, position, movement, and other spatial properties. Minds are not extended; their essence is *thinking*. For Descartes, thinking included not only ordinary thinking, but feeling, perceiving, imagining, dreaming, intending, and anything we think of as involving consciousness.

Cartesian dualism is now referred to as a form of *substance dualism*. But the word "substance" is used in different ways by different philosophers, including Descartes. In the phrase "substance dualism" as used in modern philosophy of mind, it simply means the view that the mind and body are regarded as fundamentally different kinds of *things* as opposed to fundamentally different sorts of properties of the same thing, as property dualists maintain (see below).

Cartesian dualism is sometimes called *interactive dualism*. Not all substance dualists agree with Descartes that the mind and body causally interact. Occasionalists, most notably Nicolas Malebranche (1638–1715), hold that all events are caused directly by God, so mental events and physical events not only do not interact, but they also don't even cause events of the same kind. Worldly events are the occasion for God to create other events, but do not cause those other events. Parallelists, most notably Leibniz (see below), hold that God has created a preestablished harmony among events, giving the illusion of mutual causation.

Property dualism, the position mainly discussed in the dialogue, maintains that although there is just one substance involved— the mind is, basically, the brain—that one substance has two very different kinds of properties, mental and physical. David Chalmers explains and provides arguments for property dualism in his influential book *The Conscious Mind*.

Epiphenomenalism. In ordinary use, an epiphenomenon is an accompaniment of a condition or situation of interest that is somehow secondary in importance. In discussions of the mind and body problem, it has acquired a more determinate sense. An epiphenomenon is something that is *caused* by a physical state or event, but does not itself have any physical effect. *Epiphenomenalism* is the view that mental events like experiences are epiphenomenal. If you grab a red-hot poker, the events caused by the heat on your hand will cause physical events in your brain, and these will in turn cause a severe experience of pain. Intuitively, that pain in turn causes physical events, such as letting go of the poker and screaming. But, on the epiphenomenalist view, that is an illusion. Those events are also caused by the family of physical events that caused the pain, but the pain played no part. It is an epiphenomenon. An epiphenomenalist doesn't need to maintain that the epiphenomenal events are themselves nonphysical; there could be physical events that have no physical effect, or at least ones that are relevant. But the epiphenomenalist is more typically a dualist who seeks to explain how nonphysical properties and events can be postulated without violating the principle that physical events have only physical causes, which is usually assumed in physical science.

Fallacy of misplaced negation. Suppose you don't know whether you will have salad or coleslaw for dinner. Then you do *not* know that you will have coleslaw. But it doesn't follow that you know that you will *not* have coleslaw. To suppose that it follows is to commit the fallacy of misplaced negation.

This is not a fallacy people are likely to commit when the issue is salad or coleslaw. But sometimes, in complicated philosophical discussions, the fallacy is tempting. At the beginning of his *Meditations*, Descartes argues that he can doubt that his body exists but can't doubt that his mind does—he can't doubt that he exists as a thinking being. So he does *not* know that his mind is his body or a part of it. He is sometimes accused of inferring from that that he knows that his mind is *not* his body or a part of it, which would be to commit the fallacy. The accusation is, however, not quite fair, as Sam Miller points out in the dialogue.

Indiscernible. In ordinary use, "discernible" means perceptible, and "indiscernible" means roughly "can't be discriminated on the basis of perception." But in philosophy the word has acquired a special meaning, due to Leibniz' principle of "the identity of indicernibles," which states that if A and B have all of their properties in common, they are identical, one and the same. Here the properties are not limited to perceptible properties. Leibniz' principle is controversial; less controversial is its converse, the indiscernibility of the identical: if A and B are identical, one and the same, then they have all of their properties in common.

Materialism and physicalism. These terms are often used as synonyms. Strictly speaking, however, *materialism* is the view that the world consists of material objects—that is, substances that have mass and occupy space, the smallest of which are atoms. However, physicists have come to recognize that there is more to the physical world than matter: there is energy, there are waves as well as material things, there are subatomic phenomena, studied in quantum physics. In this dialogue, *physicalism* is the view that whatever the ultimate principles and phenomena physics postulates as necessary to explain rocks, planets, human bodies, and other paradigmatically physical phenomena turn out to be, they will also be sufficient to explain everything else, including mental phenomena. However, the best way to characterize physicalism is itself an ongoing philosphical issue.

Monads. In the philosophy of Gottfried Leibniz (1646–1716), the basic units of reality are monads, simple indivisible entities that act in predetermined ways in coordination with all the others monads in a "pre-established harmony." This harmony means that the monads behave as if they were affected by and affecting a common world, but there is really no interaction between them; the ordinary world of things is mere appearance.

Necessary conditions, sufficient conditions, and INUS conditions. Let A and B be conditions in a broad sense: states, events, or properties. If it is true that B implies A, then B is *sufficient* for A, and A is *necessary* for B. That is, if you have B, you must, in some relevant sense, have A. Thus, the presence of oxygen is necessary for human survival, and human survival is sufficient for the presence of oxygen. Having 180 interior degrees is necessary for a plane figure to be a triangle, so being a triangle is sufficient for being a plane figure having 180 interior degrees. Being colored is necessary for being red, so being red is sufficient for being colored. If studying is a necessarry condition for getting a perfect score on the exam, getting a perfect score on the exam is a sufficient condition for having studied. The sort of necessity involved is causal in the first example, logical in the second, perhaps metaphysical in the third, and practical (and also causal) in the last.

In the case of causation, however, things are a bit more complicated. The terminology usually suggests that the necessary or sufficient condition is a causal factor, occurring earlier than, or at least simultaneously with, that for which it is necessary or sufficient, usually thought of as a result. So while studying for an exam may be causally necessary for getting a perfect score on the exam, it would be odd to say that getting a perfect score was causally sufficient for studying, without further explanation of what one has in mind.

It is natural to think of the causes of an event as individually necessary and jointly sufficient for the event. J. L. Mackie pointed out, however, that this is not quite correct. Consider the example of the examination. When we say that studying is a necessary condition for getting a perfect score, we have a certain scenario in mind. Smith is an honest student, taking an exam of some difficulty from an honest teacher. If Smith is reasonably intelligent, has a good memory, does not freak out in exam situations, studies hard, and has a bit of luck, she will get a perfect score. The conditions are individually necessary and jointly sufficient, or so we say.

But if we think about it, there are other sets of jointly sufficient conditions. If the teacher has the exam, along with the answers, stored on his computer, a dishonest Smith could get a perfect score without studying, by hacking into the teacher's computer, downloading the information, and copying the answers on her forearm. Or perhaps the teacher is dishonest, and any student can get a perfect score by buying the answers ahead of time, again without studying.

There are really different sets of jointly sufficient conditions: studying, being reasonably intelligent, remembering, not panicking, and being a bit lucky; or having a teacher who puts the exam and answers on a computer, hacking, and writing the information on one's forearm; or having a dishonest teacher and paying the price for the exam ahead of time. And there are indefinitely many other scenarios, like having an absurdly easy exam and being pretty lucky.

So what is the status of studying? Mackie would say it is an INUS condition. This means that studying by itself is *insuf-ficient*. Without a good memory, lack of exam-phobia, and a little luck, it won't get you a perfect score. But it is a *necessary* part of *that* set of jointly suffient conditions. (Mackie sometimes says "nonredundant" instead of "necessary.") That set isn't itself necessary since there are the other scenarios. That is, the set as a whole is *u*necessary. But although not *uniquely* sufficient, it is *s*ufficient. So studying is an *i*nsufficient condition that is a *n*ecessary part of a set of conditions that is *u*necessary but *s*ufficient for achieving a perfect score on the exam—in other words, an *INUS* condition.

Other minds problem. The philosophical problem of other minds is simply how we know that other minds exist. In the context of this dialogue, how do I know that you are not a zombie, a being who behaves much like I do, but has no experiences? It seems we know of our own experiences directly; we are directly aware of them as they occur. But I don't experience your pain, or what goes on, if anything, in your mind. What reasons do I have for believing you have experiences, and are those reasons good enough for my belief to count as knowledge?

A common, but controversial, account is *the argument from analogy*. You and I are basically similar in all sorts of ways. We have similar bodies, and we have good observational reasons for thinking that the bodies and brains of all people are organized and "wired" in similar ways. We are very similar systems. Arguments from analogy reason from similar causes to similar effects in similar cases. We both grab a red-hot poker. We both drop it and scream. Physically we are similar systems. In my case, I observe an experience of intense pain. It seems reasonable that what happens in your case is analogous.

But compare this case. The employees' parking lot at the Ford dealership is occupied by fifteen blue 2017 Ford Focus automobiles. They are completely similar in every observable way. One of the cars is unlocked. You look inside and see a box of Kleenex on the floor, tucked under the front passenger seat. You infer that the other fourteen cars also have a box of Kleenex in the same position.

This seems like a very shaky inference. You are reasoning from one observed case to fourteen others. It seems as likely or more likely most of the other cars have no such box of Kleenex. Why is the argument from analogy any better? I am the only person with an unlocked mind, or at least with one that is unlocked for me. I find experiences in it. Is this a solid reason for believing that there are experiences in the minds of the billions of other people on Earth?

Suppose, however, that you look under the hood of one of the cars and find a gasoline engine suitably connected to a transmission, driveshaft, axles, and wheels. You stay around long enough to note that all the cars leave the parking lot under their own power at closing time, and all emit the sound of a working gasoline engine. If you are sure that the gasoline engine powers the car from the hood of which you opened, it seems a much safer bet than the one concerning the Kleenex box that the same thing is going on in the other cars. That is, if you have a *causal* theory about how the one car works that depends on the observed engine, and explains the behavior is shared with the fourteen other cars, it seems pretty plausible that the same theory applies to the others. It's not certain; perhaps some of the cars are electrically powered and equipped to make the sound of a gasoline engine. But it's a much stronger hypothosis than the one about the Kleenex box.

This is why the problem of other minds may present a special problem for the epiphenomenalist. If experiences are epiphenomena, they don't really explain the behavior that other people share with you. Perhaps the fact that you have experiences is just an accident, a singularity. The argument from analogy without a causal theory to back it up seems weak, but the epiphenomenalist, it seems, can offer nothing better.

Physical correlate of a thought. Dualists and physicalists may agree that events in the brain are correlated with thoughts, sensations, and other mental phenomena. Physicalists maintain that the correlated brain event *is* the mental event, while dualists maintain that the brain event is at most *the cause of* the mental event.

Preemption and overdetermination. Suppose Elwood is driving for the basket. Sondra and Sam are guarding. They both jump high, and both swat the ball, and as a result Elwood misses. Sondra's swat and Sam's swat are each powerful enough to dislodge the ball from Elwood's hands without the other. If the swats hit the ball simultaneously, we have a case of *overdetermination*. The swats together dislodged the ball, but either on its own would have sufficed. If Sondra's swat hits the ball and disloges it before Elwood swats it, then Sondra's swat has *preempted* Sam's as the cause of the missed basket. Sondra's swat caused the ball to be dislodged, Elwood's did not, but it would have, had Sondra's swat not occurred first.

Intuitively, in the case of preemption we have a cause that is not an INUS condition (see above), for Sondra's swat wasn't necessary; Sam's would have done the job. However, if we take the N in INUS to mean "nonredundant" rather than "necessary," a change Mackie made, we would still have an INUS condition. Sondra's swat was a nonredundant part of the combination of actual factors that led to Elwood missing the shot. That is, other factors, by themselves, wouldn't have led to Elwood's missing.

Primary qualities. Galileo, Descartes, Locke, Newton, and other philosophers and scientists recognize a distinction between primary and secondary qualities; the terminology is due to John Locke. *Primary qualities* are the basic qualities of material objects that are involved in being extended and having position and movement in space and time. Primary qualities include shape, size, position, motion, and distance. But, according to Locke, many qualities we ordinarily take to be properties of material objects are merely *powers* to produce changes in other objects. Those that are powers to produce sensations in minds are *secondary qualities*. For example, redness is not really a property of an apple or a fire hydrant in the same way that its size or shape is. Redness is basically a property of sensations in the minds of humans and other animals with color vision. When we say that an apple is red, we mean simply that the apple has the power, in virtue of the primary qualities of its parts, to cause red sensations in us and other animals with suitable visual systems when we look at them in the right conditions—for example, when there is light. Smells, tastes, sounds, and temperatures are also regarded as secondary qualities.

Locke also recognizes qualities that like secondary qualities, are powers to produce changes in other objects, not limited to minds, in virtue of primary and secondary qualities. For example, the sun has the power to melt wax, and flowers have the power to attract bees.

Raw feels and qualia. "Raw feels" was Herbert Feigl's term for the basic phenomena of experience in *The "Mental" and the "Physical."* In more recent discussions, the term "qualia" is often used.

Both terms are associated with Thomas Nagel's phrase "What is it like" from his seminal paper "What Is It Like to Be a Bat?" Nagel argued persuasively that it must be like something to be a bat—that is, to fly around navigating by sonar. There must be a fact of the matter, and it is at least not obvious and indeed seems unlikely that it could be a physical fact. Studying the physical facts involved in the bat's ability to use sonar wouldn't seem to tell us what it is like to be a bat using sonar; it seems like it would have to be bats, or at least be possessed of batlike powers of navigation by sonar, to know what it is like to be a bat. Nagel's paper contained the seeds of the knowledge argument, and it was a major stimulus to a revival of philosophical interest in consciousness as a problem for various forms of physicalism.

Souls. In many religious traditions, the soul, or *psyche*, is the immaterial, spiritual core of a person, closely connected with, or identical with, the mind. The soul is regarded as the ultimate locus of moral responsibility, the proper object of praise and blame, reward and punishment. Souls are usually regarded as *immortal*—that is, the soul does not end when the body it inhabits ceases to live. In traditional theology, after death of the body the soul is transported to heaven or hell, or perhaps purgatory, depending on its level of sinfulness or goodness. Thus, the apparent injustice of earthly life, where the wicked often prosper and the good often suffer, is compensated for in the grand scheme of things.

Zombies and vampires. Zombies and vampires are species of *undead* beings—that is, humans who have died but whose corpses have somehow been reanimated in troublesome forms. *Zombies* come from Haitian folklore, and typically survive on human flesh; *vampires* come from Europe. Vampires leave their graves at night and drink the blood of the living. In the present author's opinion, both are fictional.

Philosophical zombies are also fictional, but they are not so unpleasant; as a rule they neither eat human flesh nor drink human blood. They are allegedly possible beings, like humans in every physical respect, but with no qualia, raw feels, or, in the way the word is used in the dialogue, experiences. The *zombie argument* holds that since there *could* be a being exactly like a given human in every physical respect but with no experiences, experiences must not be physical phenomena. The argument is developed by David Chalmers in *The Conscious Mind*.